AWESOME OCEANS
AMAZING ANIMAL
JOURNEYS

Michael Bright

FRANKLIN WATTS
London · Sydney

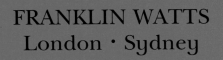

Produced by:
Aladdin Books Ltd
28 Percy Street
London W1T 2BZ

ISBN 0-7496-4746-9

First published in
Great Britain in 2002 by:
Franklin Watts
96 Leonard Street
London EC2A 4XD

Editor:
Kathy Gemmell

Designers:
Flick, Book Design & Graphics
Simon Morse

Illustrators:
Mike Atkinson, Roy Coombs,
Ian Moores, Richard Orr,
Steve Roberts – Wildlife Art,
Chris Shields, Stephen Sweet –
SGA, Ian Thompson, Ross
Watton – SGA, Norman Weaver
Cartoons: Jo Moore

Photograph credits:
All photographs courtesy of
Digital Stock.
Picture researcher:
Brian Hunter Smart

Contents

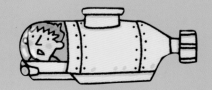

Introduction

Some of the animals that swim below or fly above the waves undertake the longest migrations on the planet. Many go between feeding and breeding sites, taking advantage of good seasonal conditions at both ends of the journey. Some do not feed at all when travelling, while others follow 'highways' in the ocean, where they gorge on plentiful plankton and small fish. Exactly how they find their way is still a mystery, but their journeys are not random. They all know precisely where they are going.

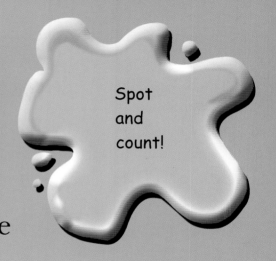

Spot and count!

Q: Why watch out for these boxes?

A: For answers to the animal journey questions you always wanted to ask.

zoom in on...

Bits and pieces

These boxes take a closer look at the features of certain animals or journeys.

Awesome facts

Watch out for these puffin diamonds to learn more weird and wonderful facts about ocean animals and their extraordinary journeys.

Interconnecting oceans

All the world's oceans are linked together, yet animal travellers rarely venture from one ocean to another, even those that migrate long distances. Some ride ocean currents as they sweep around landmasses. This helps them to travel further using less energy and also to reach their destinations accurately.

Bull sperm whales (see page 12) spend the summer in Antarctic waters feeding on giant squid, but they head north in winter. Off the Pacific coast of South America, they follow the icy, fish-rich Humboldt Current all the way to the Equator, where they join females off the Galápagos Islands.

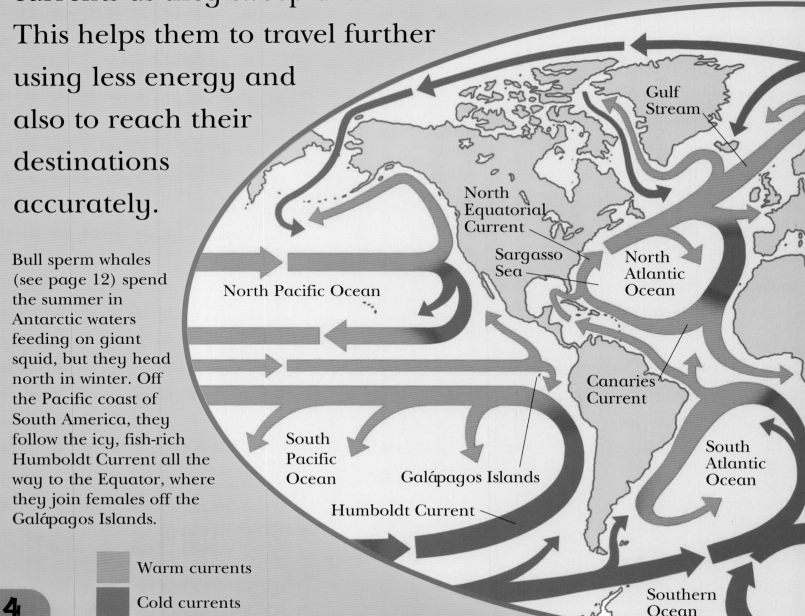

Gulf Stream

North Equatorial Current

Sargasso Sea

North Atlantic Ocean

North Pacific Ocean

Canaries Current

South Pacific Ocean

Galápagos Islands

Humboldt Current

South Atlantic Ocean

Southern Ocean

Warm currents

Cold currents

4

Common eels (see page 19) mature in European and North American rivers, then head for the sea to breed. They follow the clockwise circulation of currents in the North Atlantic to reach their spawning grounds in the Sargasso Sea.

Q: Why do some animals migrate long distances?

A: They travel to where food is most abundant at particular times of year. Many marine animals, for example, travel to the edge of polar seas in summer. Here, plankton blooms and there is a superabundance of fish and squid. Others have to travel because the distance between their traditional feeding and breeding sites has increased enormously as the continents have slowly moved apart over millions of years (see page 14).

Arctic Ocean

North Pacific Ocean

Indian Ocean

South Pacific Ocean

Blue whales (see page 8) in the eastern Pacific regularly travel north and south between California and Costa Rica. In the north, they feed on the swarms of krill that gather at upwellings along the Californian coast. In the south, it is thought that they gather at mating and calving grounds off Central America.

Both male and female blue sharks (see page 13) frequent the eastern coast of North America, but only females are found in the mid-Atlantic. They are heading for Europe and the Mediterranean, where they will have their young.

5

Common dolphins in the Gulf of California travel from one side of the Gulf to the other, depending on the direction of the wind. They head for whichever coast has the wind blowing away from the shore. The wind causes upwellings of nutrients which are fed on by plankton and fish.

zoom in on...

Different sizes of migrant

Animals of all sizes migrate. The largest animal in the world, the blue whale, swims to and from tropical seas, where it breeds, to feeding sites in the temperate and polar seas. Krill, the small shrimp-like creatures that the blue whale eats, also 'migrate' – not across the water, but up and down. They rise towards the surface every night to eat, then sink down during the day to avoid their predators.

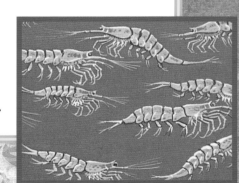

Making journeys

Animal journeys in the sea can be long or short, across the water or up and down. Some jellyfish that live around South Pacific islands swim a short distance across their saltwater lake each day just to stay in the sun, while the Australian 'mutton bird' flies a figure-of-eight route over the entire Pacific Ocean in search of food over the year.

Male southern elephant seals fight over females at their traditional breeding beaches on sub-Antarctic islands, but they swim many kilometres to the edge of the pack ice to feed. They make regular vertical migrations between the surface, where they go to breathe, and the deep sea, where they hunt.

Whale ways

All the large whales travel the oceans, some swimming great distances. Scientists now use radio tags tracked by satellites to follow whales and find out where they go. But still some species – even the biggest – keep their destination a secret. Blue whale breeding sites, for example, are still unknown.

There are several separate populations of humpback whales in the Atlantic and Pacific Oceans, both in the northern and southern hemisphere, but they never meet. In summer, the whales go to their nearest temperate or polar seas to feed on the seasonal abundance of food. In winter, they fast and head back to the tropical seas to breed.

to eat tiny shrimp-like animals buried in mud on the sea floor.

zoom in on...

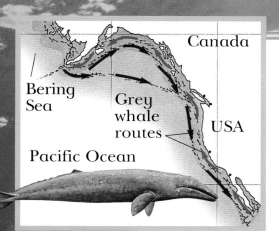

Bering Sea

Canada

Grey whale routes

USA

Pacific Ocean

Grey whales

Grey whales travel the greatest distance of any mammal. They swim close to shore along the Pacific coast of North America, from breeding sites in the lagoons of Baja California to feeding sites in the Bering Sea on the northern Alaskan coast. Not all whales go all the way, but nobody knows why.

Equator

Humpback migration

→ Winter

Summer

Sea signals

Groups of migrating animals need to communicate with their companions. Whales make very low-frequency sounds that can travel hundreds of kilometres. The sound vibrations bounce between layers of water of different densities and temperatures.

Q: Which whale sings?

A: Male humpback whales sing when they reach their breeding grounds. The songs are the longest of any animal, including birds, and can last for half an hour. In a single population, the songs are constantly changing, but all the whales keep up to date with the latest version and sing the same song.

High-frequency sounds do not travel far through water, so only sea creatures in tight groups, such as porpoises and these Atlantic spotted dolphins, use high frequencies to talk to each other and co-ordinate group movements. Many species have distinctive call signs, with every member of a certain school or pod producing the same call.

zoom in on...

Low-frequency contact

Fin whales travel the ocean in a group that might spread over several kilometres. They stay in contact using sounds that are even lower than the lowest note on a piano. If one whale calls, the others answer.

Ocean currents

Marine migrants often use ocean currents to help them travel more quickly and use less energy. Blue sharks in the North Atlantic hitch a ride on the fast-flowing Gulf Stream, for example, and cover about 35 km per day.

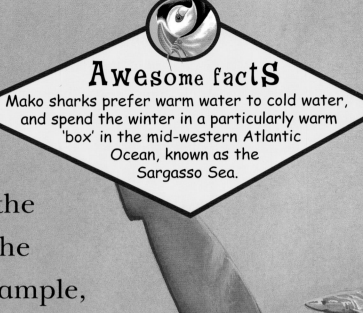

Awesome factS

Mako sharks prefer warm water to cold water, and spend the winter in a particularly warm 'box' in the mid-western Atlantic Ocean, known as the Sargasso Sea.

zoom in on...

Travelling in cold water

While many migrants in the northern hemisphere swim in warm-water currents, bull sperm whales in the southeast Pacific follow the icy Humboldt Current to and from the Antarctic and the Equator (see page 4). This is because ocean currents on the western side of continents in the southern hemisphere are very rich in food.

Young female blue sharks in the North Atlantic mate off New England, then head immediately for Europe. They mature on the way, with blue shark babies developing inside their body. They follow the Gulf Stream to Spain, Portugal and the Mediterranean, where they give birth. Afterwards, they join the southward-flowing Canaries Current, then finally hitch a ride on the North Equatorial Current back to America (see page 4).

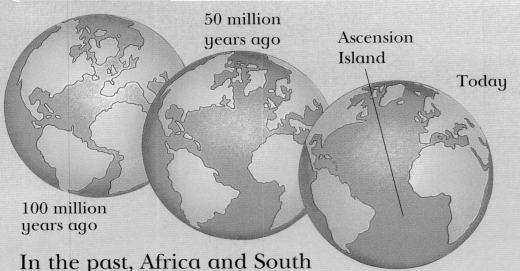

100 million
years ago

50 million
years ago

Ascension
Island

Today

In the past, Africa and South America were much closer. Over millions of years, the continents drifted apart. This may explain a very long journey made by Brazilian green turtles. They ignore suitable breeding beaches in Brazil and migrate instead all the way to tiny, mid-Atlantic Ascension Island – which would once have been much closer – to breed.

The first hazardous journey for thousands of green turtle hatchlings on Costa Rican beaches is the scramble to the sea. Waiting predators, such as black vultures, iguanas, ghost crabs and frigate birds, seize and eat the tiny turtles. The survivors disappear into the sea, only to return four or five years later to the same beach to breed.

Q: Where do leatherback turtles travel?

A: Leatherbacks are the largest turtles and most widely distributed reptiles in the world. One population travels from breeding beaches off South America all the way to temperate seas off Scotland, where they hunt jellyfish. They swim at great depth, following the continental shelf off the USA's Atlantic coast, then the Gulf Stream all the way to northern Europe.

body warmer than sea water, so it can swim in cool seas.

Turtle travel

Sea turtles are great
travellers. Loggerhead turtles,
for example, travel between their
egg-laying beaches around the South China Sea
and their feeding grounds off California. They follow
a food-rich 'superhighway' across the Pacific Ocean,
where plankton, jellyfish, crustaceans and fish gather.

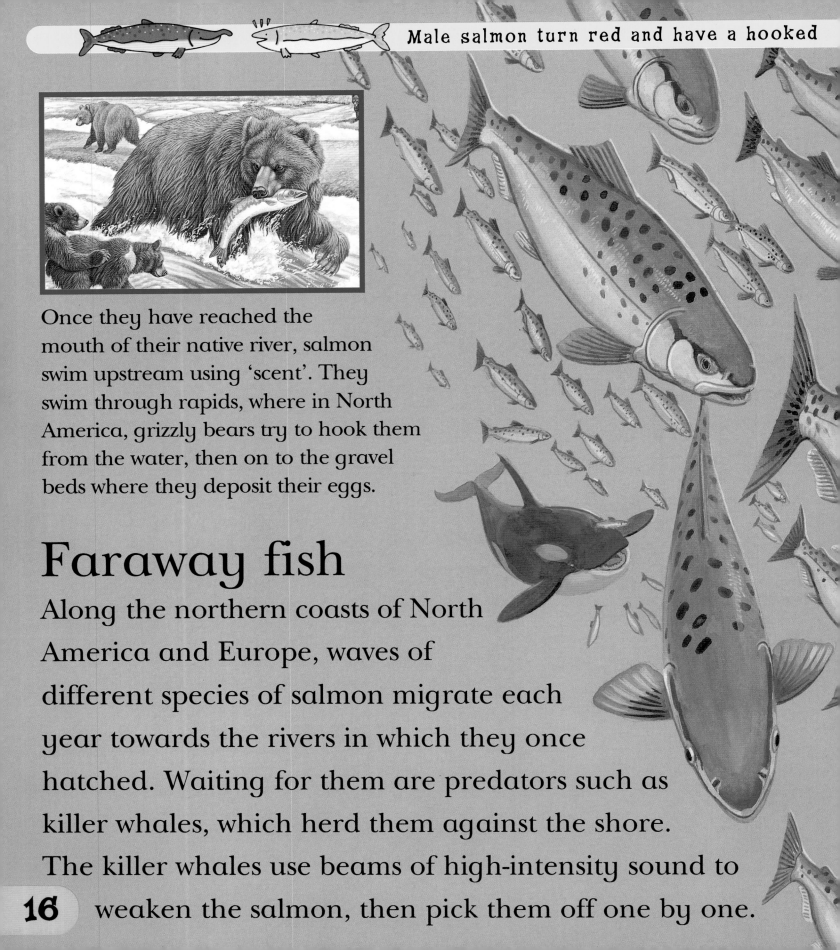

Once they have reached the mouth of their native river, salmon swim upstream using 'scent'. They swim through rapids, where in North America, grizzly bears try to hook them from the water, then on to the gravel beds where they deposit their eggs.

Faraway fish

Along the northern coasts of North America and Europe, waves of different species of salmon migrate each year towards the rivers in which they once hatched. Waiting for them are predators such as killer whales, which herd them against the shore. The killer whales use beams of high-intensity sound to

16   weaken the salmon, then pick them off one by one.

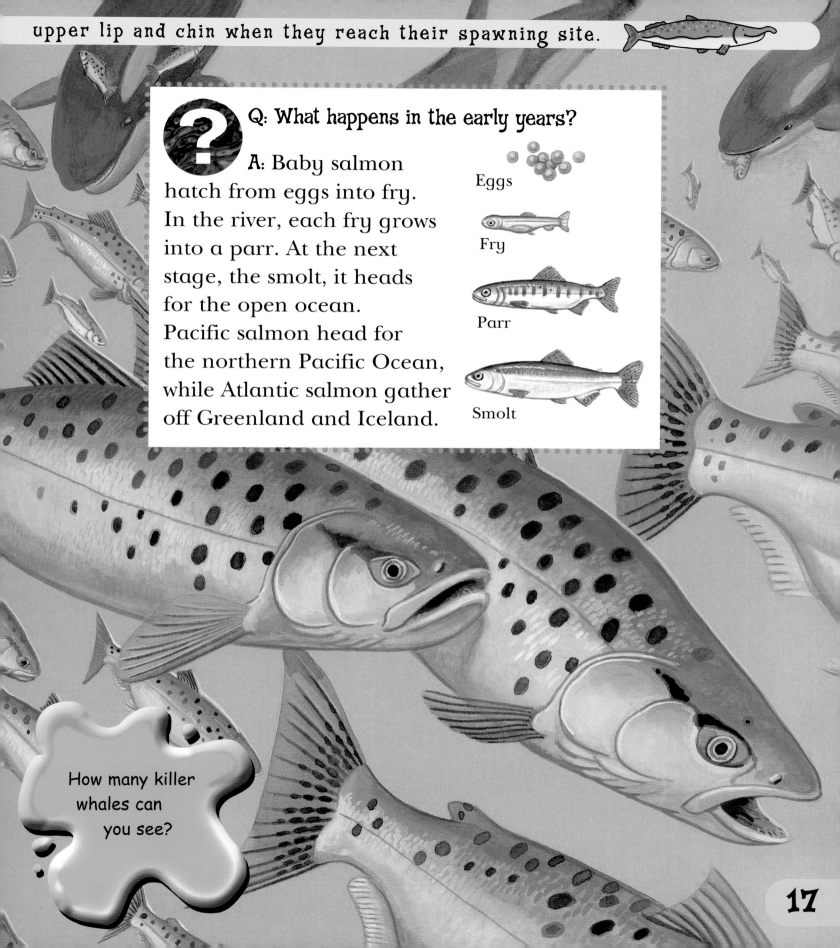

Q: What happens in the early years?

A: Baby salmon hatch from eggs into fry. In the river, each fry grows into a parr. At the next stage, the smolt, it heads for the open ocean. Pacific salmon head for the northern Pacific Ocean, while Atlantic salmon gather off Greenland and Iceland.

Eggs

Fry

Parr

Smolt

How many killer whales can you see?

Eel journey

1. Eel eggs hatch and small leaf-shaped larvae emerge. These set off for estuaries on either side of the Atlantic. They take a year to reach North American rivers and three years to reach Europe. The larvae gradually metamorphose (change shape) on the way.

zoom in on...

Metamorphosis

Like an eel, a butterfly changes shape as it grows in a process called metamorphosis. A butterfly begins life as an egg, which hatches into a caterpillar. The caterpillar may build a cocoon, or chrysalis, where it changes into a full-grown butterfly.

Caterpillars

Butterfly

3. The mature eels swim all the way back to the Sargasso Sea to spawn, and then they die.

18

Amazing eels

The common eel makes several amazing journeys in its lifetime. It spawns in the Sargasso Sea in the North Atlantic, but for much of its life it lives in rivers and streams in North America and Europe. It can adapt to salt water and fresh water at different stages in its life cycle.

2. When the eel larvae reach the coast, they become transparent elvers, or glass eels, and enter fresh water. After their first summer, they turn into yellow eels, as their back becomes dark green and their belly yellow. After about seven years in lakes or rivers, they change into mature silver eels and return to the sea. The head becomes streamlined and the eyes grow bigger.

Going together

Some animals migrate together in extraordinary numbers. Off the east coast of South Africa, sardine shoals several kilometres long migrate northwards from the Cape of Good Hope. This annual 'sardine run' takes place during winter in the southern hemisphere, between June and September.

Tuna

Between March and September, when the tide is high on Californian beaches, fish called grunion migrate inshore by the thousand. They ride in on the surf, deposit eggs in the sand, then leave on the next wave. The eggs develop in the damp sand and the young hatch at precisely the time of the next very high tide, when they are washed out to sea.

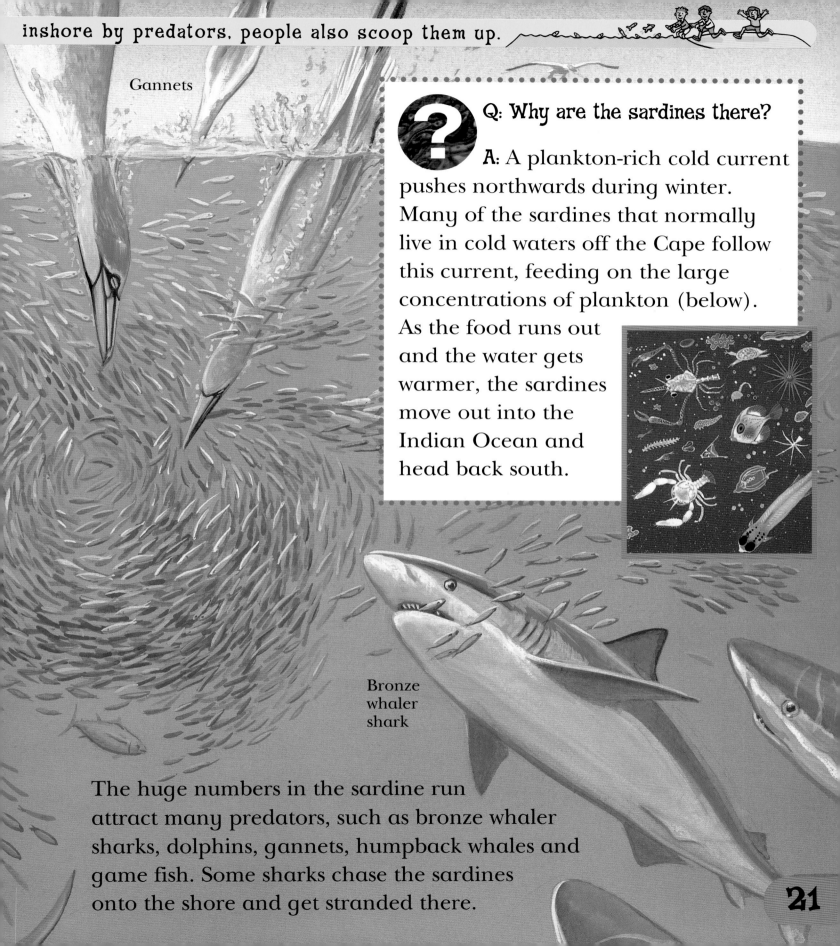

Gannets

Q: Why are the sardines there?

A: A plankton-rich cold current pushes northwards during winter. Many of the sardines that normally live in cold waters off the Cape follow this current, feeding on the large concentrations of plankton (below). As the food runs out and the water gets warmer, the sardines move out into the Indian Ocean and head back south.

Bronze whaler shark

The huge numbers in the sardine run attract many predators, such as bronze whaler sharks, dolphins, gannets, humpback whales and game fish. Some sharks chase the sardines onto the shore and get stranded there.

21

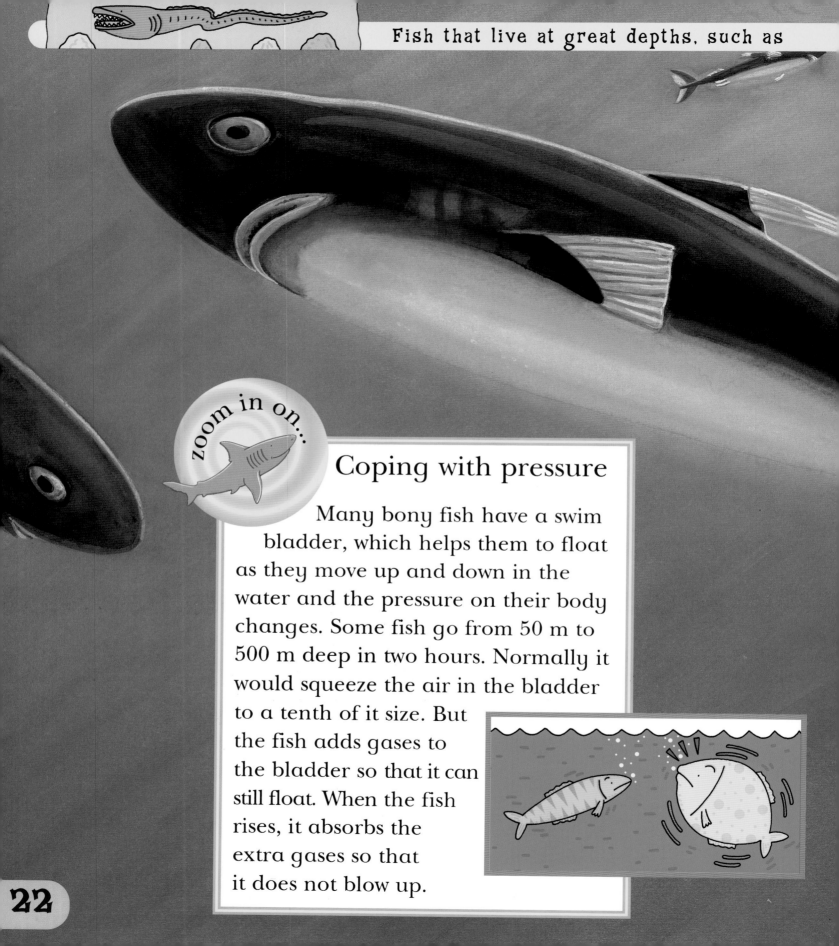

zoom in on...

Coping with pressure

Many bony fish have a swim bladder, which helps them to float as they move up and down in the water and the pressure on their body changes. Some fish go from 50 m to 500 m deep in two hours. Normally it would squeeze the air in the bladder to a tenth of it size. But the fish adds gases to the bladder so that it can still float. When the fish rises, it absorbs the extra gases so that it does not blow up.

Up and down

Some deep-sea animals embark on a daily journey from the depths, where they spend the day, to the surface to feed at night. They follow the zooplankton, which make a similar journey. Some fish travel as far in relation to their size as a person who runs a marathon before breakfast and dinner every day.

The dwarf shark is just 15 to 25 cm long, yet it travels 200 m or more on its daily vertical migration from the ocean mid-waters to the surface. It has luminous organs along its belly. When seen from below, the shark is virtually invisible against the background glow from the surface. The shark has to adapt to changing temperatures: the water in the depths is a chilly 10°C, but at the surface it can be as warm as 27°C.

23

Running the gauntlet

As if the atrocious weather and sea conditions were not bad enough, penguins returning to their nests also have to run the gauntlet of various predators. Killer whales and leopard seals patrol near the shore, and bull southern sea lions chase them on the beach. At the nest site, birds like skuas and caracaras swoop out of the sky, picking off the weak and the injured.

The emperor penguin is the only creature that has its young during the Antarctic winter. The male looks after the egg and then the newly hatched chick, balancing it on its feet under protective folds of skin until the spring, when the female returns from feeding at sea. Over the next few months, the pair takes turns to care for the chick and travel the 200 km or so across the ice to feed in open water.

24

Awesome facts
Emperor penguins 'sledge' rather than walk when travelling on ice. In this way, they move at 4.5 km/h and can cover great distances using the minimum of energy.

Perilous passage

Animal travellers in the Southern Ocean have a tough time. Winds, waves and ocean currents swirl furiously around the Antarctic, throwing penguins about as if they were in a washing machine. However, adult penguins still have to make their way between their nest sites and the ocean. Their chicks depend on them returning safely.

Arctic terns travel the greatest distance of any animal. They fly between the Arctic and Antarctic each year – an annual round trip of 40,000 km. In autumn, they fly south along the Atlantic coasts of either North and South America or Europe and Africa.

zoom in on...

Nesting sites

Manx shearwaters nest in burrows, which they drop into at night, making blood-curdling shrieks and cries. The adult birds make extensive journeys from their nesting sites along the western coast of Britain to the Atlantic coast of South America, where they spend the winter.

Above the waves

Seabirds, such as terns, albatrosses and shearwaters, embark on enormous journeys in order to find food. Some fly from one end of the world to the other, which means that they are in almost year-round sunlight and can make the most of the concentration of fish that feed on the summer plankton blooms.

How many Arctic terns can you see?

Short-tailed shearwaters 'fly' underwater to catch their food, but they must travel great distances to find it. They nest on islands off Tasmania, then spend the next seven months on the wing searching for fish. They cover 32,000 km per year, in a figure-of-eight flight path over the entire Pacific Ocean. They use the prevailing winds at each leg of the journey to minimise the amount of energy they use.

Some animals have tiny grains of a substance called magnetite attached to nerve endings in their head or neck. The magnetite reacts to the Earth's magnetic field (below), like the iron in a compass needle. This activates the nerves and provides the animal with a kind of internal compass so that it can work out in which direction it is going.

Q: How do birds use the sun and stars?

A: To use the sun as a useful navigational tool, migrating animals must be able to appreciate its apparent movement across the sky. Some night-flying birds use the light from the setting sun to work out which direction they should set off in, so even though the sun is below the horizon, its light can still be a navigational aid. During the night, the main navigational sign in the northern hemisphere is the North Star. The chicks of migrating birds, such as Arctic terns, can often be seen staring at the sky, looking at the constellations (above) that they will use later in life.

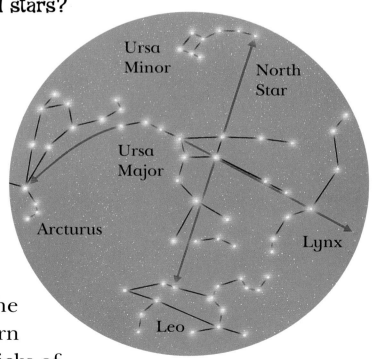

Finding the way

On long-distance journeys, many birds navigate using the sun, moon and stars. As they get closer to their destination, they often rely on landmarks. Many have remarkable back-up systems they use when the sky is cloudy. They can also detect and respond to the Earth's magnetic field.

How many white albatrosses can you see?

Before heading out to sea, newly fledged puffins fly around their nesting burrows to familiarise themselves with local landmarks. This helps them to find the way back to the nesting site after their feeding journeys.

29

Long-distance problems

Migrating animals face many dangers, some caused by human activity. Sandbar sharks, for example, migrate between New York and Mexico, a distance of some 3,000 km each way. They are often caught along the route by fishing fleets. Because the sharks are slow to mature and have few young, their population is now declining.

Wandering albatrosses scour the Southern Ocean for squid and fish to bring back to their rapidly growing chicks. They use up-draughts to gain height, then glide back towards the sea's surface. They may find an easy meal in discarded fish from boats using long fishing lines, but many get caught in the lines and drown.

zoom in on...

Bluefin tuna

Bluefin tuna migrate from the Mediterranean to the Atlantic coast of Norway each year, taking about a month to complete the journey. Shoals of 10,000 tuna used to travel through the Straits of Gibraltar, but overfishing has caused the population to crash. This means that Mediterranean fishermen have destroyed their own livelihood.

Glossary

Crustacean
A hard-bodied animal with no backbone but with many hanging body parts that have a variety of functions, from eating to walking.

Equator
An imaginary line around the centre of the Earth, midway between the poles.

Hemisphere
Either half of the world, split horizontally by the Equator.

Krill
A shrimp-like crustacean that lives in huge swarms at the ocean surface.

Larva
A young stage in certain animals' development that looks nothing like the adult form. Plural: larvae.

Migration
The movement of animals to and from particular areas, such as feeding and breeding grounds. Animals that migrate are called migrants.

Nutrient
Any nourishing foodstuff.

Plankton
The tiny plants and animals that live at the surface of the sea. Animal plankton is called zooplankton.

Polar seas
Seas close to the Arctic and Antarctic.

Population
A group of individuals of the same type.

Predator
An animal that hunts and eats other animals.

Prevailing wind
The wind that blows most often from a particular direction.

Radio tag
A small radio device that is attached to animals. It transmits a signal that can be followed by a scientist on foot or tracked by a satellite in space.

Reptile
A backboned animal with scales that lays eggs, such as a turtle. Reptiles are cold-blooded: their temperature varies with their surroundings.

Species
Animals that resemble one another closely and are able to breed together.

Swim bladder
The gas-filled, balloon-like organ in the roof of the abdomen of a bony fish that enables the fish to float in the water.

Temperate seas
The seas between the tropics and the poles.

Tropical seas
Seas in the tropics – the hot areas of the world on either side of the Equator.

Upwelling
The rising of water from the ocean depths, often bringing a rich supply of nutrients to the surface.

Index